A Merry Little Christmas

A Merry Little Christmas

12 Popular Classics for Choirs

COMPILED AND EDITED BY
Jerry Rubino

MUSIC DEPARTMENT

OXFORD
UNIVERSITY PRESS

OXFORD
UNIVERSITY PRESS

198 Madison Avenue, New York, NY10016, USA
Great Clarendon Street, Oxford OX2 6DP, England

Oxford University Press is a department of the University of Oxford.
It furthers the University's aim of excellence in research, scholarship,
and education by publishing worldwide

Oxford New York
Auckland Cape Town Hong Kong Karachi
Kuala Lumpur Madrid Melbourne Mexico City Nairobi
New Delhi Shanghai Taipei Toronto

With offices in

Argentina Austria Brazil Chile Czech Republic France Greece
Guatemala Hungary Italy Japan Poland Portugal Singapore
South Korea Switzerland Thailand Turkey Ukraine Vietnam

Oxford is a registered trademark of Oxford University Press

5 7 9 10 8 6 4

ISBN 0–19–386639–0   978–0–19–386639–3

Music and text origination by
Barnes Music Engraving Ltd., East Sussex, England

Printed by Halstan & Co. Ltd., on acid-free paper

CONTENTS

PREFACE

The wonderful music in this collection combines two distinct (and too often diverse) objectives: to be artistically challenging as well as popular and entertaining. I was first asked to create arrangements of this caliber when I was on the staff of the Dale Warland Singers, a professional vocal ensemble in the Twin Cities of Minneapolis and St. Paul. I am thrilled that Oxford University Press has agreed that this standard should become common among the broader genre of choral music!

Flavoring some of the best-known holiday tunes, the top-level arrangers of *A Merry Little Christmas* were told *not* to simplify their work but rather to challenge the choral ensemble. With swinging rhythms, expanded harmonic interest, and intense piano parts, these arrangements fulfill exacting and challenging artistic standards and will result in performances that excite audiences everywhere.

Instructions from a printed page of music can only provide part of what it takes to sing successfully. To capture the meaning of the text and the sound of the style, one must integrate an emotional response to the text with musical elements to achieve a fun, dramatic, and honest sound. Each arranger has provided separate performance notes, but here are some general suggestions for "pop music performance practice": Pop music sometimes requires a tone more horizontal, less vertical in approach. Emotion is a critical component of performance, so expression should not only include dynamics and articulation, but also facial expression, body movement, and individual expression!

The arrangements in this exciting collection vary, and therefore so will the performance practices. I encourage you to enjoy the process of discovery so that this form of vocal music, one that originated in the United States, may thrive and be a significant source of repertoire that educates and entertains.

JERRY RUBINO
Minneapolis, Minnesota, USA

COMPOSER BIOS

Greg Jasperse
Greg Jasperse is a composer, arranger, recording artist, and educator currently living in Chicago. As a commissioned composer, he has written for the American Boychoir, Chicago Children's Choir, and Kokopelli (Edmonton, Canada). He is a frequent clinician for various festivals and choir and jazz camps in the US and Canada. In addition he serves as musical director for musical theater productions and cabaret artists. He is assistant conductor of the Lakeside Singers, a 24-voice ensemble of professional singers in Chicago.

Paul Johnson
Paul Johnson has enjoyed a 30-year career in music, producing dozens of albums, three of which were nominated for Grammy Awards. His choral arranging, with its characteristically tight harmonies, has received much praise. Johnson has composed five full stage musicals, including *Red Red*, which received the third prestigious European "Musical of The Year Award." He served as arranger and musical director for the American Cinema Awards Show in Beverly Hills, CA for seven years working with Whitney Houston, Al Jarreau, The Four Tops, Petula Clark, Michael Bolton, Andy Williams, and many more. His Christmas classic, "Christmas Is The Best Time Of The Year", was featured in the Radio City Music Hall Christmas Show in New York City for nine seasons.

Bob Krogstad
Bob Krogstad's career in music spans nearly four decades. During this time he has composed and arranged choral and instrumental music for leading publishers around the world. He served as Musical Director for both the late jazz great, Mel Tormé and Natalie Cole. His love of Christmas music can also be found on the five albums he recorded with the London Symphony for Hallmark Cards.

Paul Langford
Paul Langford is a Chicago-based freelance musician, involved in all aspects of live and recorded music. His background in choral music encompasses a lifetime of singing and writing for the full range of amateur to professional singing groups. Paul received his BM in Conducting from Oklahoma Baptist University in 1984, under the tutelage of Michael Cox.

David Maddux
David Maddux has arranged, orchestrated, and composed music in a variety of settings for over three decades. His choral revues have featured Harvey Fierstein, Rosemary Clooney, Lily Tomlin, Lesley Gore, Frederica Von Stade, Armistead Maupin, Ann Hampton-Callaway, Judith Martin ("Miss Manners"), and Nell Carter. His *a cappella* jazz vocal production, "An Evening In December," was nominated for a Grammy Award.

Kevin Robison

Kevin Robison's work has been commissioned, performed, and recorded by choruses around the United States. He is also known in the theater world for his innovative approach to singing from an actor's perspective and has written a book about his process. His arrangements have been performed by Susan Egan, Malcolm Gets, Jenifer Lewis, Joanna Gleason, and Lily Tomlin. Robison is the Artistic Director of South Coast Chorale and serves as Assistant Conductor of Gay Men's Chorus of Los Angeles.

Jerry Rubino

Jerry Rubino holds degrees in piano, music education, and conducting from Temple University and the University of Minnesota. He currently serves as Minister of Music at Spirit of Hope United Methodist Church in Golden Valley, Minnesota. Rubino worked for 23 seasons with the Dale Warland Singers, as associate conductor, director of special projects and music education, pianist, singer, and arranger. In 1983, at the request of the Minnesota Orchestra, Rubino formed the Warland Cabaret Singers, now Jerry Rubino Plus. Under his direction, they developed a unique sound and style and became known for their crossover programming and educational outreach. He serves as repertoire and standards chair of vocal jazz for the North Central Division of the American Choral Directors Association and is requested nationally as a choral clinician, music director, pianist, and adjudicator.

Vijay Singh

Vijay Singh is an active teacher, composer, arranger, and performer residing in Ellensburg, WA where he is Associate Professor of Jazz and Choral Music at Central Washington University. His student ensembles at CWU have been honored as some of the finest in the nation, and he has guest conducted All-State Jazz and Concert Choirs in over a dozen states. He is well known for his eclectic versatility and for his diverse compositions, arrangements, and performances in both choral and jazz idioms.

Michele Weir

Michele Weir is on the faculty at UCLA, a former member of the Grammy-nominated "Phil Mattson and the PM Singers," and an internationally respected jazz educator, arranger, and vocalist. Recent notable presentations include the World Choral Symposium, the ACDA National Conference and the IAJE Convention. Michele's arrangements are widely published and have been performed by many groups such as Beachfront Property, New York Voices, M-Pact, Chanticleer, The Boston Pops, and the Pacific Symphony. She has authored books on Vocal Improvisation, Jazz Singing, and Jazz Piano Basics. In addition, Michele served as music supervisor for the foreign-language dubs of the Dreamworks film, "Prince of Egypt."

PERFORMANCE NOTES

1. Blue Christmas
This arrangement emulates the sound of vocal groups from the 1950s. Characteristic of this style, accompanying *oos* should have almost as much personality as the melody. Not quite as croony as the approach of vocal groups from the 1940s, this style should sound cool, connected, and classy.

2. A Christmas Love Song
The dynamics and tempi markings are suggestions, but feel free to allow your own interpretation based on the lyrics and musical flow to personalize your choir's performance. Beware of allowing too much vibrato during thick divisi harmonies, keep the vowels bright and speech-like, and sing with energy to the end of every phrase and articulation. The *doos* in the introduction and final few measures should be thought of as "instrumental textures," sung with purity and bell-like clarity; when the lyrics enter, allow the text and natural syllabic stress to guide your interpretation.

3. Feliz Navidad
This arrangement should be performed with light but supported voices. Relaxed vowels and consonants should reflect how one would speak the text in conversation, rather than a more formal, choral approach. Singers should smile and raise their eyebrows, not only to keep the tuning centered and the tone light, but also to communicate the levity and celebration of the song. The tempo should be rock steady without sounding metronomic or rigid, and syncopations should sound relaxed, rather than over-worked or labored. Though not drastic, a raised dynamic level or two at the chorus each time will provide the necessary excitement and a welcome contrast to the verse.

4. Have yourself a merry little Christmas
In this *a cappella* setting remember that you are instruments in a vocal band, charged with the task of teasing out the rich harmonic colors. *Oos* and *ahs* should sound like string pads. *Do doots*, in a ballad like this, should simulate muted brass and French Horns. Begin strong, with an attitude that says, "Quiet everybody. Listen to this!"

Here, as in other arrangements with close harmonies, avoid uncontrolled vibratos within the same chord. Memorize your note as if it were the melody, even if it's not. There's a certain kind of magic that happens when voices lock in together on a cool, tight chord. In rehearsal, hold these chords and feel how they sound. It's a good way to train your ear how to hear the chord, how to tune it up, and how to enjoy it.

On the unison lines, think of your voice like Velcro adhering to the voice next to you. Listen to each other, sing together, breathe together, and be careful not to drag the tempo.

5. I'll be home for Christmas

The harmonic structure is progressive, with definite jazz influences, requiring a tone that is even and effortless. The voice-leading is designed to make the intricate and complex harmonies accessible. The *ostinato* in the accompaniment at m. 22 is meant to invoke a feeling of sentimental longing, and the *crescendo* out of that pattern at m. 36 is crucial to the piece's unfolding. The tall chords beginning in m. 92 should be quiet, rich, and lush.

6. It's the most wonderful time of the year!

Throughout the arrangement, keep a bright smile going across the choir, reflecting the joy of the season. This will not only enhance the tone of the choir, but will also match the spirit of the lyrics. Note that the dynamic needs to be full, but not loud throughout most of the song. When it does achieve a *forte*, it should be done with great fervor. But remember to keep it happy in spirit! When you reach the 4/4 section at m. 115, turn on that Broadway gusto. The rests are placed exactly where I want you to breathe, so always sing the full value of the notes.

7. Rudolph, the red-nosed reindeer

To capture the drama in this arrangement, keep the tempo up to at least $\quarternote = 126$. After the piece is learned, you can take it even faster if you dare! It is designed to be comedic at times, for example at m. 4, and mm. 55–75, so don't be afraid to have some fun with it! Pay careful attention to the distribution of parts for the best possible balance throughout the piece, adding or deleting voices as necessary. For example, the melody needs to stand out prominently from the background vocals when it enters at m. 17, and the Soprano and Alto parts at mm. 38 and 102 should be evenly balanced.

The bass part is the driving force underneath the rest of the choir and is designed to emulate the sound of an acoustic jazz bass. It's vital that there are enough singers assigned to this part for it to be heard adequately. It should be sung assertively and in a steady, driving tempo. The syllable *dm* should have a strong attack in the beginning of the word, then a sustained *m* sound immediately following with *no vowel sound at all*. Passages with the syllables *da ba da ba* should be sung *legato* with clear articulation on the accented notes and should have a strong sense of forward motion. To help these lines flow naturally, allow the vowel to modify somewhat from "ah" as in "father" to "uh" as in "fun." For short notes where the syllable *dat* appears, use a bright, speech-like, and elongated "ah" vowel.

8. Santa Claus is coming to town

To retell this beloved tale successfully, you must enter into the text and make it come alive. Let the harmonic tensions and releases in the opening four measures dictate how to maximize the rubato marking. Off-beat entrances should always have a "lean" to them—not so much an accent but a weight that is countered by the inner pulse from which the entrance responds.

The *doo*s in the bass at m. 7 imitate an acoustic bass guitar. Incorporating a decay on each note will facilitate imitating that sound. The "t" on the *doot*s beginning at m. 41 are imploded and meant to stop the sound of each quarter note. I considered using dots over the notes but want to avoid any kind of accent on this accompanying figure. Most of the piece should be sung without vibrato, the exceptions are when the singers have the melody and at the end of phrases.

When the men and women move to two-, three-, and sometimes four-part writing, it is best to put equal numbers of singers on each note. The balance of the individual notes in these chords is vital to the harmonic excitement of the arrangement.

9. We need a little Christmas

This arrangement should have the energy of Ethel Merman without necessarily her vocal tone! Instead of putting accents on each of the notes, place a little decay from notes that often begin phrases. For example in the opening phrase, the first two notes should have attacks that decay a bit and then *crescendo* through the repeated notes in mm. 9–10 to the juicy chord in m. 11. Each phrase should have shape in accordance with key words in the text, the shape of the tune, and harmonic movement. From m. 76 to the end, the sound of the music should match the drama of the lyrics! The piano playing should be aggressive without rushing.

10. We wish you a merry Christmas

The opening *fa la la*s are easy and should give you just enough time to tune yourself up, find your balance, and then execute mm. 3–4 with confidence. Remember to turn the vibrato off when singing tight harmonies.

Since you're singing "We wish you…" over and over, give a good accent on the downbeat (on the word "wish") each time. Sell this notion to the audience. Every time you sing the *fa la la*s your whole voice and face should light up as though you just plugged in the Christmas tree. Turn on the wonder and magic over and over again.

On the "cluster busters"—that is, tight harmonies—you have to concentrate a little harder. Learn and sing your part with confidence as if it were the melody. Be just a little bit sassy knowing that you've got the cool note. Almost oversell "and a Happy New Year" at the very end, and it should turn out perfectly.

11. What are you doing New Year's Eve?

This arrangement emulates the sound of vocal groups from the 1940s. Sing each phrase very smoothly, making the most of the shape of the musical line as would an instrumentalist. It is important that the whole group feel the eighth-note swing together to make this number sound authentic.

12. Winter Wonderland

Perform this arrangement with a steady tempo and an even sixteenth-note feel, so that the result is a gentle groove. I suggest a conversational approach to the diction. Sing how you speak. To counterbalance the fairly rhythmic piano part, sing with flow and direction on the long vocal phrases. Make the tone fairly straight in the places where there's more harmonic tension. Vibrato is more appropriate at the ends of the phrases and once the chords are lined up and tuned. In the piano part, keep the sixteenth notes even. In order to achieve the contemporary feel, accent beats one and three. Give a small accent to some of the sixteenth-note offbeats, especially if they happen right before beat one or three.

1. Blue Christmas

BILLY HAYES and JAY JOHNSON
arr. David Maddux

25

me. And when those   blue   snow-flakes   start   fall - in',

me. And when those blue, when those blue_   snow - flakes_ start fall - in',_____

me. And when those blue, when those blue   snow-flakes   start   fall - in',

And when those   blue, when those blue   snow-flakes   start   fall - in',_____

Ped.   Ped.

29

that's when those   blue   mem-'ries   start   call - in'._____

that's when those blue   mem - 'ries_ start   call - in',   call - in'._

that's when those blue,   lone-ly blue mem-'ries   start   call - in',   start

that's when those blue,   lone-ly blue mem - 'ries_ start   call - in'._____

Ped.   Ped.   Ped.

2. A Christmas Love Song

Alan and Marilyn Bergman

JOHNNY MANDEL
arr. Vijay Singh

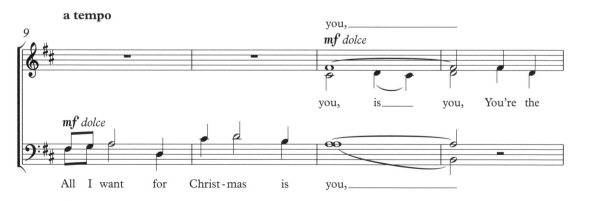

Broader

Christ - mas__ this__ is,'__ Long be - fore__ the snow - flakes_ ap -

- pear, ap - pear, With-out balls or mis-tle - toe_____ or the

tin-sel's sil-ver glow You just look at me and 'Oh__ Christ-mas is__

here, it's here!' You just look at me and 'Oh Christ-mas is

Tempo primo

doo_ doo_ doo_ doo
here!' doo_ doo_ doo_ doo
doo doo doo doo

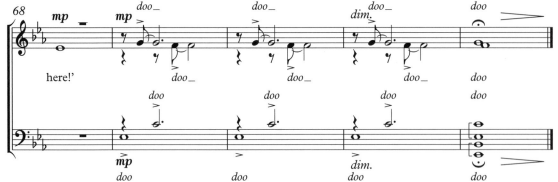

doo doo doo doo

for the Caroling Party

3. Feliz Navidad

JOSÉ FELICIANO
arr. Paul Langford

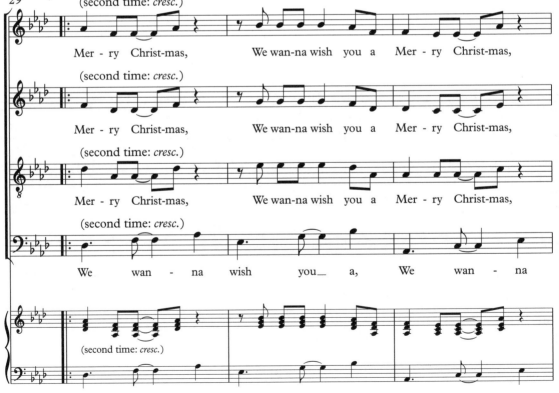

4. Have yourself a merry little Christmas

RALPH BLANE and HUGH MARTIN
arr. Paul Johnson

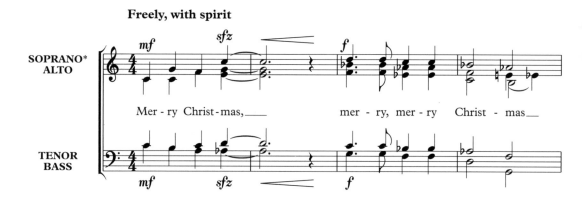

* SATB subdivided into six parts, evenly balanced.

5. I'll be home for Christmas

KIM GANNON and WALTER KENT
arr. Kevin Robison

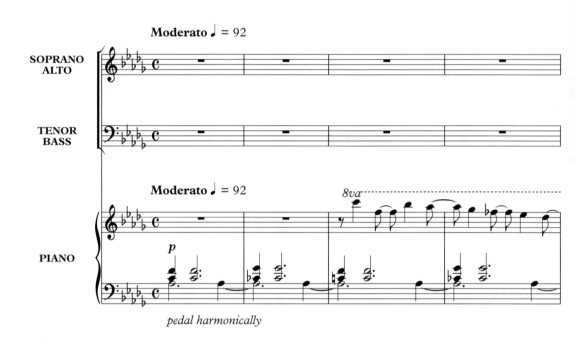

6. It's the most wonderful time of the year!

GEORGE WYLE and EDDIE POLA
arr. Bob Krogstad

toast-ing, and car-ol-ing out in the snow; lu___ lu___

There'll be scar-y ghost

unis.

lu lu___ lu___ lu oo_____

stor-ies and tales of the glo-ries of Christ-mas-es long, long a-

ah_____ It's the most

unis.

- go._____ It's the

7. Rudolph the red-nosed reindeer

JOHNNY MARKS
arr. Michele Weir

* The melody should be allocated to a small group of women with optional men an octave lower. Balance of parts should be taken
into careful consideration when assigning parts. (Optionally, melody can be sung by a soloist on microphone.)

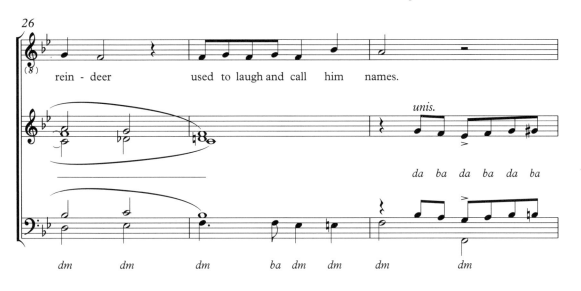

* for all quarter notes with the syllable, 'dat', use a bright, speech-like and elongated 'ah' vowel.

** Regardless of previous allocation of melody parts, use a small group of women and men an octave lower for bars 59-70b.

8. Santa Claus is coming to town

Haven Gillespie

J. FRED COOTS
arr. Jerry Rubino

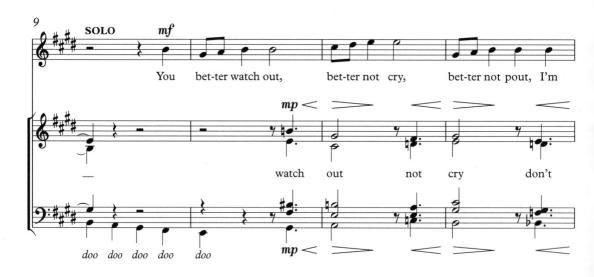

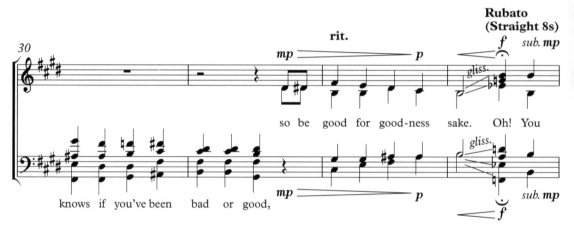

doot   doot   doot   doot   doot   doot   doot   doot   doot   doot   doot   doot   doot   doot   doot   doot

lit-tle tin horns,   and   lit-tle toy drums,   Roo-ty toot toots and   rum-my tum tums,

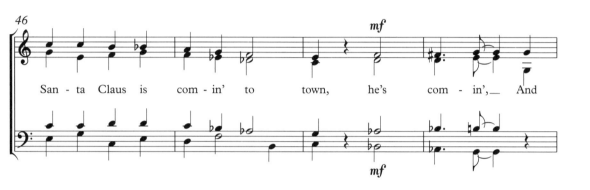

San - ta   Claus   is   com - in'   to   town,   he's   com - in',___ And

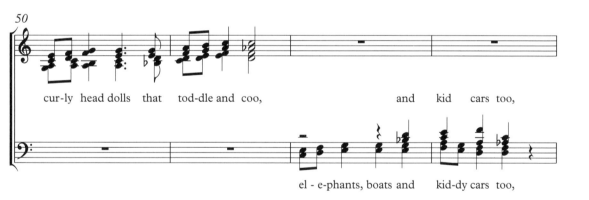

cur-ly head dolls   that   tod-dle and coo,   and   kid   cars too,

el - e-phants, boats and   kid-dy cars too,

town._____   The

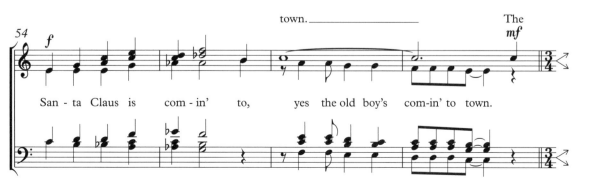

San - ta   Claus   is   com - in'   to,   yes   the old boy's   com-in' to town.

* Keyboard reduction for rehearsal only.

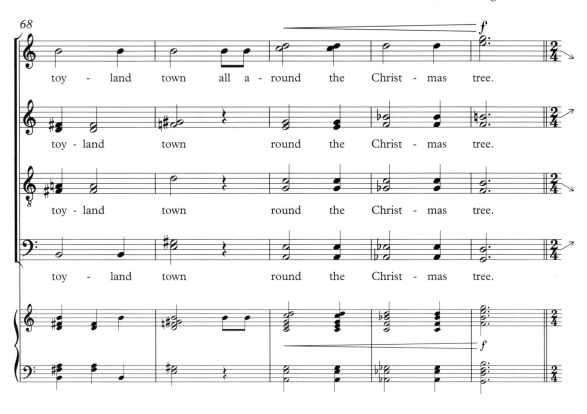

* Keyboard reduction for rehearsal only.

9. We need a little Christmas

JERRY HERMAN
arr. Jerry Rubino

up   the   stock - ing;   We may be   rush - ing   things   but

deck the   halls___   a - gain   now.___

deck the   halls___   a - gain   now,   deck the halls   now.

deck the   halls___   a - gain   now,   deck the halls   now.

deck the   halls___   a - gain   now,   deck the halls   now.

For we need a lit-tle Christ-mas right this ve-ry min-ute, Can-dles in the win-dow, Car-ols at the spi-net, yes, we need a lit-tle Christ-mas right this ve-ry

min - ute.   It   has - n't snowed a   sin - gle   flur-ry but   San - ta,   dear, we're

in   a   hur-ry so

Climb   down   the   chim - ney,   turn on the

Slice   up   the

bright - est   string   of   lights I've ev - er   seen.

fruit - cake; It's time we hung some tin - sel on that ev -

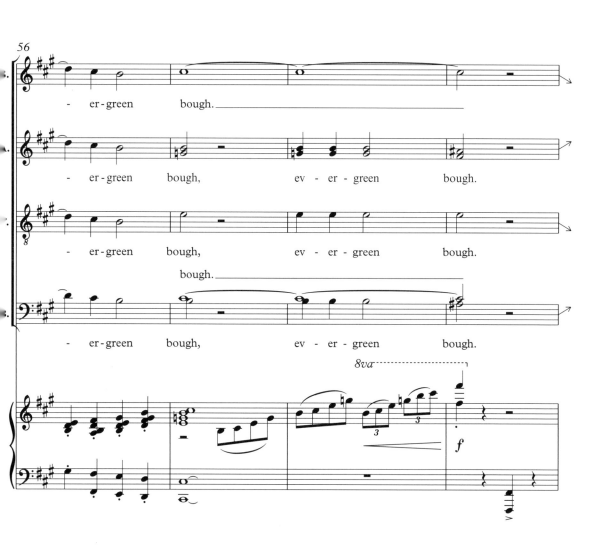

- er - green bough._____

- er - green bough, ev - er - green bough.

- er - green bough, ev - er - green bough.

bough._____

- er - green bough, ev - er - green bough.

10. We wish you a merry Christmas

English Traditional
arr. with new lyrics by Paul Johnson

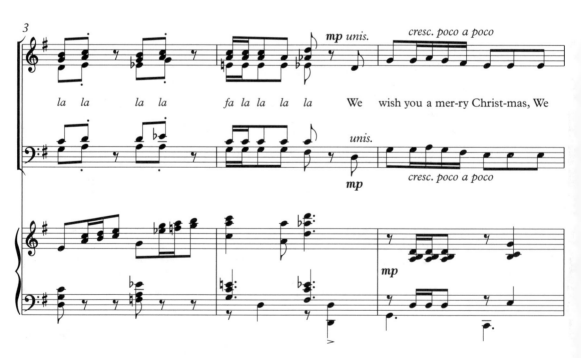

11. What are you doing New Year's Eve?

FRANK LOESSER
arr. David Maddux

ques - tion_ in ad - vance: what are you do - ing New Year's,

ques - tion in ad - vance: what are you do - ing,_____ do - ing New Year's,

ques - tion_ in ad - vance: what are you do - ing,_____ do - ing New Year's,

ques - tion_ in ad - vance: what are you do - ing New Year's, New,

ques - tion_ in ad - vance: what_ are you do - ing New_ Year's,

New Year's Eve? What are you do - ing_____

New,_ New Year's Eve, New Year's Eve?_ What are you do - ing_

New Year's Eve?_____ What are you

New Year's Eve?_____

New Year's Eve?_____

12. Winter Wonderland

Richard B. Smith

FELIX BERNARD
arr. Greg Jasperse

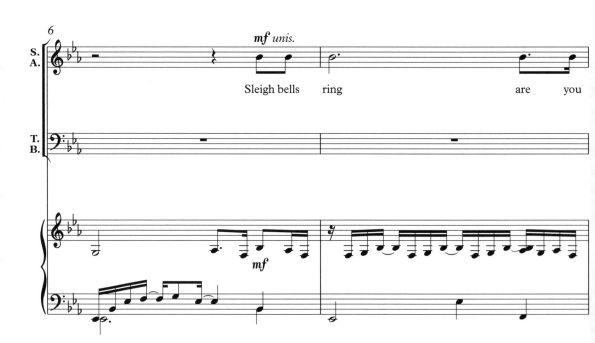

snow - man,   And pre-tend that he is Par - son

Brown;   He'll say 'are you mar-ried?' we'll say 'No_ man,   But

you can do the job_ when you're in   town.'   La - ter